The Countries

Egypt

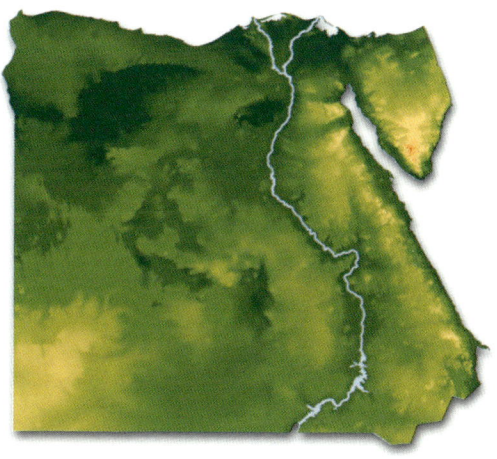

Bob Italia
ABDO Publishing Company

visit us at
www.abdopub.com

Published by ABDO Publishing Company, 4940 Viking Drive, Edina, Minnesota 55435. Copyright © 2001 by Abdo Consulting Group, Inc. International copyrights reserved in all countries. No part of this book may be reproduced in any form without written permission from the publisher.

Printed in the United States.

Photos: Corbis, AP/Wide World
Editors: Tamara L. Britton, Kate A. Furlong, and Christine Fournier
Art Direction & Maps: Neil Klinepier

Library of Congress Cataloging-in-Publication Data

Italia, Bob, 1955-
   Egypt / Bob Italia.
      p. cm. -- (The countries)
   Includes index.
   ISBN 1-57765-493-5
    1. Egypt--Juvenile literature. [1. Egypt.] I. Title. II. Series.

DT49 .I83 2001
962--dc21

2001016123

Contents

Ahlan! 4
Fast Facts 6
Timeline 7
Ancient History 8
The Land 14
Plants & Animals 18
The People 20
The Economy 24
Cities 26
Transportation 30
Government 32
Holidays & Festivals 34
Fun in Egypt 36
Glossary 38
Web Sites 39
Index 40

Ahlan!

Hello from Egypt! Egypt was one of the greatest civilizations of the past. The ancient Greeks saw Egypt as the source of all wisdom. Roman emperors traveled to Egypt to marvel at monuments such as the pyramids. The worship of Egyptian gods and goddesses spread through the Roman Empire as far as Great Britain.

Many of Egypt's ancient towns, temples, and tombs have been unearthed. Egypt has more ancient ruins than any other country in the world!

In the Nile Valley, the past seems very close. The people who lived there thousands of years ago left a lasting legacy of art, architecture, and literature.

Ahlan *from Egypt!*

Fast Facts

OFFICIAL NAME: Arab Republic of Egypt
CAPITAL: Cairo

LAND
- Highest Peak: Jabal Katrinah 8,651 feet (2,637 m)
- Major River: Nile
- Major Deserts: Western Desert, Eastern Desert
- Major Lake: Nasser

PEOPLE
- Population: 68,359,979 (2000 est.)
- Major Cities: Cairo, Alexandria, Giza
- Official Language: Arabic
- Official Religion: Islam

GOVERNMENT
- Form: Republic
- Head of State: President
- Head of Government: Prime minister
- Legislature: People's Assembly
- National Anthem: "Beladi, Beladi" ("My Country, My Country")
- Independence: 1922

ECONOMY
- Agricultural Products: Corn, cotton, oranges, potatoes, rice, sugarcane, tomatoes, wheat
- Manufactured Products: Chemicals, cotton textiles, fertilizers, processed foods, steel
- Mining Products: Petroleum
- Money: One pound equals one hundred piasters

Egypt's Flag

A bill worth 50 piasters

Timeline

3200 B.C.	Upper and Lower Egypt unite
2614-2502 B.C.	Egyptians build the Pyramids and Sphinx
332 B.C.	Alexander the Great conquers Egypt for the Greeks
A.D. 1798	France controls Egypt
1801	England seizes control of Egypt
1805	Muhammad Ali takes control of Egypt
1850-1869	Suez Canal built
1879	England regains control of Egypt
1922	Egypt gains independence
1953	Egypt becomes a republic
1967	Six-Day War with Israel
1979	Egypt and Israel sign the Camp David Accords

Ancient History

Egypt has one of the world's oldest civilizations. It began more than 5,000 years ago. At first, Egypt was divided into Upper and Lower Egypt. King Menes united them around 3200 B.C.

Dynasties ruled Egypt until 30 B.C. During Egypt's early dynasties, kings were considered gods. The king's family held all positions of power. People built pyramids as tombs for kings, to keep them happy in the afterlife.

Under King Amenhotep III (ah-men-HO-tep), ancient Egyptian civilization reached its peak. Foreign trade was strong. The cities of Thebes and Memphis became the political, commercial, and **cultural** centers of the world.

But in 332 B.C., Alexander the Great easily conquered Egypt for the Greeks. He founded the city of Alexandria. It became the intellectual center of the world.

Ancient History **9**

The Great Pyramids at Giza were built between 2614 and 2502 B.C.

In 30 B.C., the Romans conquered Egypt. Christianity spread throughout the land. Then, for hundreds of years, Egypt was ruled by other strong empires. It was ruled by Persians, Byzantines, Muslim Arabs, Ottoman Turks, and the French. In 1801, the British seized control of Egypt.

A soldier named Muhammad Ali took control of Egypt in 1805. Under his rule, the modern state of Egypt formed. From 1850 to 1869, Egyptians built the Suez Canal. The country acquired much debt.

In 1879, the British regained their control of Egypt. Then, in 1922, Britain declared Egypt independent. It became a **constitutional monarchy**.

In 1948, the **United Nations** created the new nation of Israel. It bordered eastern Egypt. Egypt disliked the creation of Israel. It fought against Israel in many wars.

An army group called the Free Officers took over the government in 1952. They felt the people were not represented fairly. In 1953, they formed a republic. Colonel Gamal Abdel Nasser became president.

Ancient History 11

Nasser wanted to make Egypt the leader of the Arab world. He made a treaty with Britain. He also started a program of **economic** and social reform.

Nasser addresses the United Nations in 1960. He is considered the father of modern Egypt.

In 1967, Israel and Egypt fought the Six-Day War. Egypt lost control of the Sinai **Peninsula**. The war crippled Egypt's **economy** and armed forces.

Nasser died in 1970. Anwar al-Sadat became president. Sadat regained the Sinai Peninsula. He also built closer ties with western countries.

In 1979, Egypt and Israel signed a peace treaty called the Camp David Accords. This angered many Arab nations. In 1981, radical Muslims assassinated Sadat. That same year, Hosni Mubarak became president. He repaired relations with other Arab countries.

In 1990, Iraq attacked Kuwait. Egypt joined the United States and other nations in a war against Iraq. During this time, religious and labor groups became violent against Mubarak. Mubarak vowed to end terrorism as he struggled with Egypt's growing population and troubled economy.

Ancient History 13

Egyptian president Anwar al-Sadat (L), U.S. president Jimmy Carter (C), and Israeli prime minister Menachem Begin (R) sign the Camp David Accords.

The Land

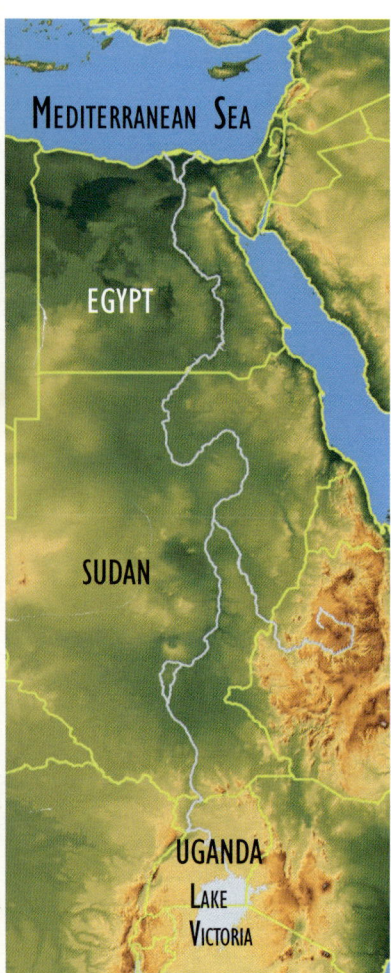

Egypt is in Africa. Egypt's land has four major regions. They are the Nile Valley and Delta, the Western Desert, the Eastern Desert, and the Sinai **Peninsula**.

The Nile Valley and Delta region follow the course of the Nile River. The Nile flows northward into Egypt from Lake Victoria. It flows through Egypt for about 1,000 miles (1,600 km).

The Nile River Delta begins at Cairo (KY-ro). The Nile Valley and Delta region contain most of Egypt's farmland.

In the southern Nile Valley is Lake Nasser and the Aswan High Dam. The dam makes electricity and supplies farms with water.

The Nile River is the longest river in the world. It flows 4,160 miles (6,695 km) northward from Lake Victoria to the Mediterranean Sea.

The Land 15

The Nile River divides Egypt into two sections. The Western Desert extends between the river and the Libyan border. The Western Desert is part of the Sahara Desert. It covers much of Egypt's total area. It is a dry **plateau** with ridges and basins.

The Eastern Desert is also part of the Sahara. It stretches to the Gulf of Suez, and the Red Sea. It is cut by **wadis** and fringed by rugged mountains in the east.

The Sinai **Peninsula** is also a desert region. Egypt's highest mountain, Jabal Katrinah, rises out of the Sinai Peninsula. It is 8,668 feet (2,642 m) high.

Egypt's climate is hot and dry through the spring and summer. Winters are mild, but it becomes cold at night. In April, hot winds called *khamsin* (kam-SEEN) blow in from the Western Desert at up to 93 miles (150 km) per hour.

Rainfall

CAIRO

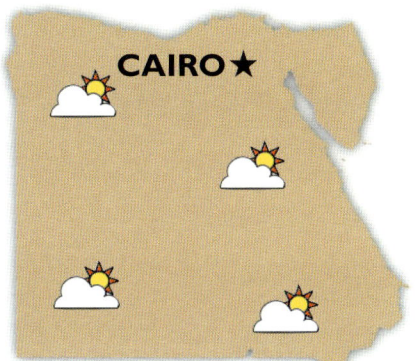

AVERAGE YEARLY RAINFALL

Inches	***Centimeters***
Under 10	***Under 25***

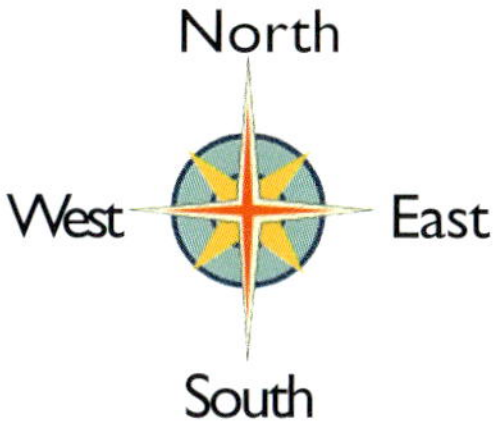

North
West
East
South

Temperature

Winter

CAIRO

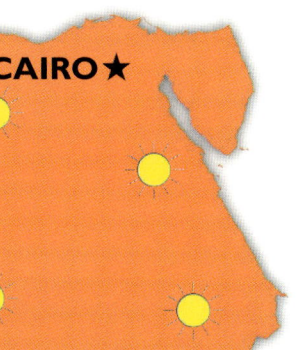

AVERAGE TEMPERATURE

Fahrenheit	***Celsius***
Over 86°	***Over 30°***
68° - 86°	***20° - 30°***
50° - 68°	***10° - 20°***

Summer

CAIRO

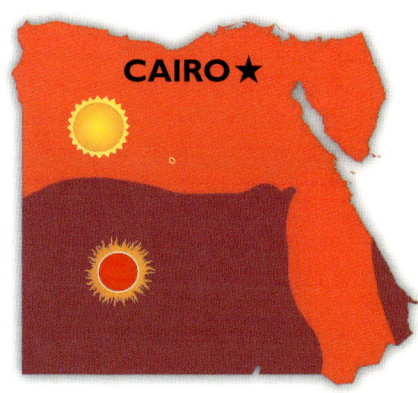

Plants & Animals

Though it gets little rain, Egypt has many kinds of plants. Wherever water exists, flowers and grasses grow. Many kinds of water plants, such as the lotus, grow in the Nile.

Egypt's deserts have tamarisk, acacia, herbs, thorny shrubs, and *markh*, a leafless tree. The country also has more than 100 kinds of grasses, including bamboo. Reeds and palm trees also grow in parts of Egypt.

Gazelles, mountain sheep, desert foxes, jackals, mountain goats, wildcats, and mongoose live in Egypt. Camels and donkeys are seen almost everywhere in the country.

A camel walks through the desert on the Sinai Peninsula.

Plants & Animals 19

Egypt has about 350 kinds of birds. Most pass through as they **migrate** from Europe to southern Africa. Egypt also has around 34 kinds of snakes and over 190 kinds of fish.

Palm trees grow in Egypt.

The People

Most Egyptians are Hamitic Arabs. They are **descendants** of the Hamites and Arabs of ancient Egypt. Egypt's main minority groups are the Nubians and the Copts. The Nubians are an African group. They live in southern Egypt. The Copts are a religious minority. They are descendants of Christian Egyptians who lived during the time of the **pharaohs**.

Islam is Egypt's official religion. Most Egyptians are Muslims. There are about six million Coptic Christians. There are also many Catholics, Protestants, and Jews in Egypt.

Arabic is Egypt's official language. Although it is spoken by all Egyptians, there are many **dialects**. Classical Arabic is used in printed materials and in schools.

Egyptians live in both urban and rural areas. The typical rural settlement is a village surrounded by cultivated fields. The villagers build their own houses out of mud bricks and straw. The flat roofs are made of dried date leaves. Urban Egyptians usually live in apartment buildings.

A rural village in southern Egypt

Girls from an Egyptian village

Many Egyptians who live in cities wear American-style clothing. Rural villagers wear traditional clothing. The men wear a long, shirtlike garment called a *galabiya* (guh-LAH-bee-uh). Women wear long, colored gowns.

Most villagers and poor city dwellers in Egypt eat a simple diet based on bread and *ful*. *Ful* is a dish made of fava beans. They also eat a dip made of chickpeas, called *hummus*. Egyptians enjoy drinking strong coffee and tea.

All Egyptian children are required to go to school from the age of 6 to 14. About half go on to secondary school. There, they can choose a general school or a technical school.

Ful Mudammas

3 pounds dried fava beans
   (soaked in water overnight)
1 large onion, chopped
Salt to taste
3/4 cup red lentils, rinsed
2 1/2 quarts cold water
2 large ripe tomatoes, chopped

Drain fava beans and add to pot of boiling water. Boil fava beans for 10-15 minutes. Remove peels. Place peeled fava beans in a pot with the onion, tomatoes, and lentils. Cover with water. Bring to a gentle boil. Skim foam off the top and reduce heat to low. Cover and cook for 12 hours. Season with salt and serve.

AN IMPORTANT NOTE TO THE CHEF: Always have an adult help with the preparation and cooking of food. Never use kitchen utensils or appliances without adult permission and supervision.

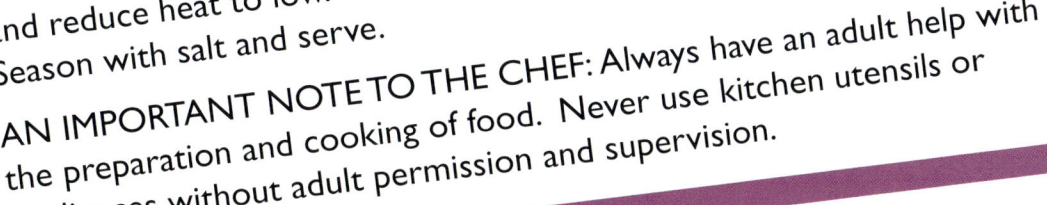

LANGUAGE

English	Arabic
Yes	Naam
No	Laa
Thank You	Shokran
Please	Min Fadlak
Hello	Ahlan
Goodbye	Ma as-salaamah
Mother	Omm
Father	Ab

The Economy

The government controls major parts of Egypt's **economy**. But the government is slowly allowing **privatization**.

Textiles and food processing are Egypt's most important industries. Egyptians also manufacture aluminum, cement, and chemicals.

Egypt also produces both oil and natural gas. The Western Desert, the Gulf of Suez, and the Sinai **Peninsula** are all rich in oil. Egyptians use most of this **petroleum**. They also sell some of it to other nations.

Agriculture in Egypt depends almost entirely on the Nile. Dams allow water to be stored for use when the river level is low. Cotton, rice, and corn are grown in summer. Barley, wheat, and beans are winter crops. Various fruits and vegetables are also grown.

Opposite page: A man works on an Egyptian oil rig.

Cities

About 68 million people live in Egypt. About half live in cities or large villages. Cairo is Egypt's capital and largest city. About 14 million people live there.

Cairo has many landmarks. The Ibn Tulun **Mosque** (mahsk) was built in the ninth century. It is one of the largest mosques in the world. The Citadel is a medieval fortress that was the seat of Egyptian power for 700 years. Cairo is also famous for the City of the Dead.

Giza, a suburb of Cairo, is on the west bank of the Nile. It is home to the Great Pyramids. They are one of the wonders of the ancient world. The pyramids were tombs for Egyptian kings. After a king died, his body was **mummified** to preserve it for the afterlife. Then the body was placed in the pyramid for protection.

Cities 27

Cairo is located along the Nile River. It is Africa's largest city.

Giza is also home to the Great Sphinx (sfehnks). A sphinx is a creature that has the body of a lion and the head of a human. Many scientists believe the Egyptians built the Great Sphinx to guard King Chephren's pyramid.

Many people also travel southeast of Cairo to the city of Luxor to see pyramids and ancient architecture. Luxor was built on the ancient city of Thebes. There, people can see the temples of Luxor and Karnak. Luxor is also the home of the Valley of the Kings.

Alexandria is Egypt's second-largest city. Alexander the Great founded the city. Along with **mosques**, Alexandria has remains of Greek and Roman architecture. Now it is Egypt's main port.

Opposite page: The Great Sphinx

Cities **29**

Transportation

Egypt has a variety of ways to get around. People can ride in cars and trucks. Camels and donkeys also share the roads. Buses serve nearly every town in Egypt.

Many Egyptians travel by train. Railways connect nearly every town in the country. Cairo has an efficient subway system as well.

Water transportation is also important in Egypt. The Suez Canal is a major link between the Mediterranean and Red seas. The Nile and its canals provide transportation for heavy goods. Tugboats, barges, and flat-bottomed boats called *feluccas* (fuh-LOO-kuhz) travel on the canals.

Many people travel to and from Egypt on airplanes. Many travelers fly into Egypt on the country's national airline, Egypt Air.

Opposite page: A man uses a donkey to haul his cart.

Government

Egypt is a **socialist democracy**. It is governed under the 1971 constitution. Islam is the state religion, and the basis of Egyptian law.

The constitution provides for a strong presidency. It also has a lawmaking body, called the People's Assembly. Out of the 444 members, about half must be farmers and workers. Members are elected for five-year terms.

The president must be nominated by at least one-third of the members of the People's Assembly. Then at least two-thirds of the Assembly must approve the nomination. Then the president must be elected by popular vote.

The government controls Egypt's communications. The Supreme Press Council supervises Egypt's magazines and its 15 daily newspapers. The government also owns and operates the country's radio and television stations.

Government **33**

Egyptian president Hosni Mubarak (C) addresses a new session of the People's Assembly on December 17, 2000.

Holidays & Festivals

Though Egyptians work hard every day, they also take time to celebrate. Egyptians celebrate religious holidays and national holidays.

Sinai Liberation Day, April 25, celebrates the return of the Sinai **Peninsula** to Egypt. Revolution Day, July 23, celebrates the day Colonel Nasser overthrew the government in 1952.

Muslims celebrate Ramadan during the ninth month of the Islamic calendar. Muslims believe that during this month, the **Koran** was revealed to the **prophet** Mohammed. Muslims fast until sunset each day. At the end of Ramadan, people celebrate with feasts and gifts.

Eid al-Adhah is the time of **pilgrimage** to Mecca. Mecca is a holy Muslim city in Saudi Arabia. Each Muslim is expected to make the pilgrimage at least once.

Coptic Christians celebrate New Year's Day, Easter, Christmas, Annunciation, Ascension, and saints' days. Both Muslims and Christians celebrate folk festivals held throughout the year.

Nomadic Bedouin men from Sinai, Egypt, prepare lamb for Id il Fitr, the feast at the end of Ramadan.

Fun in Egypt

Egyptians enjoy a variety of sports and leisure activities. Some of the most popular activities are swimming, sailing, and snorkeling. Egyptians visit beaches on the Nile River, the Red Sea, or the Mediterranean Sea.

Soccer is Egypt's national sport. Many children play on school teams. When an important match takes place, most of Cairo celebrates.

Cairo is Egypt's **cultural** center. The Coptic Museum has exhibits that cover Egypt's Christian era between A.D. 300 and 1000. Cairo is also home to the Egyptian Museum and the Egyptian National Library.

Egyptians appreciate many kinds of music. Modern Egyptian music combines folk music, traditional Arabic music, and Western music. Western-style music has been a familiar part of Egyptian musical culture since the nineteenth century.

Children play at a beach in Alexandria, Egypt.

Glossary

constitutional monarchy - a form of government ruled by a king or queen who must follow the laws of a constitution.
culture - the customs, arts, and tools of a nation or people at a certain time.
democracy - a governmental system in which the people vote on how to run the country.
descendant - a person who comes from a particular ancestor or group of ancestors.
dialect - a form of a language spoken in a certain area or by certain people.
dynasty - a series of rulers who belong to the same family.
economy - the way a country uses its money, goods, and natural resources.
Koran - a Muslim book of sacred writings.
migrate - to move from one place to another according to the seasons.
mosque - a Muslim place of worship.
mummify - to preserve a dead body in preparation for burial.
peninsula - land that sticks out into water and is connected to a larger land mass.
petroleum - a thick, yellowish-black oil. It is used to make gasoline.
pharaoh - an ancient Egyptian king.
pilgrimage - a journey to a holy place.
plateau - a raised area of flat land.
privatization - to change the ownership of a business from the government to private citizens.
prophet - a religious leader who speaks as the voice of God.
socialist - a person who believes in an economy where the government or the citizens control the production and distribution of goods.
United Nations - a group of nations formed in 1945. Its goals are peace, human rights, security, and social and economic development.
wadi - a riverbed that flows with water only after a heavy rain.

Web Sites

Egypt State Information Service
http://www.sis.gov.eg/front.htm
This site is sponsored by the Egyptian State Information Service. Visitors can read about King Tut's Tomb, modern Egyptian culture, and the latest Egyptian news. This site also has a place to listen to Egypt's national anthem and view photographs of Egyptian landmarks.

Mummies of Ancient Egypt
http://www.si.umich.edu/CHICO/mummy/
This colorful site is geared toward young readers interested in Egypt. It describes what mummies are and how they were created. This site also has information on ancient Egyptian hieroglyphics and a timeline of important events in Egyptian history.

Life in Ancient Egypt
http://www.clpgh.org/cmnh/exhibits/egypt/
This site is sponsored by the Carnegie Museum of Natural History. It has information about daily life in ancient Egypt. The site discusses mummification, gods and religion, homes, and clothing.

These sites are subject to change. Go to your favorite search engine and type in "Egypt" for more sites.

Index

A
al-Sadat, Anwar 12
Alexander the Great 8
Alexandria 8, 28
Ali, Muhammad 10
Amenhotep III, King of Egypt 8
animals 18, 19
Aswan High Dam 14

C
Cairo 14, 26, 28, 30, 36
Camp David Accords 12
Chephren, King of Egypt 28
children 22
climate 16
clothing 22

E
economy 24
education 22

F
food 22

G
geography 14, 16
Giza 26, 28
government 24, 32
Great Pyramids 26
Great Sphinx 28

H
holidays 34, 35
homes 21

K
Karnak 28

L
language 20
Luxor 28

M
Mecca 34
Memphis 8
Menes, King of Egypt 8
Mohammed 34
Mubarak, Hosni 12
music 36

N
Nasser, Gamal Abdel 10, 11, 12, 34
Nasser, Lake 14
Nile River 4, 14, 16, 18, 24, 30, 36

P
plants 18

R
religion 10, 12, 20, 32, 34, 35, 36

S
Six-Day War 12
sports 36
Suez Canal 10, 30

T
Thebes 8, 28
transportation 30

V
Victoria, Lake 14

J916.2 ITALIA
ITALIA, BOB
EGYPT

$21.35

DATE			

DISCARD

DEC 12 2001

SOUTH HUNTINGTON
PUBLIC LIBRARY
2 MELVILLE ROAD
HUNTINGTON STATION, N.Y.

BAKER & TAYLOR